Help Me To Pray

A Book of Beginning Prayers for Children

Written By Taronda Hall

Tidan Publishing LLC
P.O. Box 9482
Columbus, Georgia 31907
Tidanpublishingllc@gmail.com

Distributed by

Cover design by Tidan Publishing
Illustrations inspired by Raven, David and Cali Durant

Unless otherwise noted, all Scripture quotations are taken from the King James Bible and the New International Version, public domain.

THE HOLY BIBLE, NEW INTERNATIONAL VERSION® NIV®
Copyright © 1973, 1978, 1984 by International Bible Society®
Used by permission. All rights reserved worldwide.

Scripture quotations marked TPT are from The Passion Translation®. Copyright © 2017, 2018 by Passion & Fire Ministries, Inc. Used by permission. All rights reserved. ThePassionTranslation.com.

Published 2020
Columbus, Georgia
Printed in the United States of America

ISBN 978-1-7353208-2-3
Library of Congress Control Number: Pending

Dedicate your children to God and point

them in the way that they should go,

and the values they've learned from you

will be with them for life.

Proverbs 22:6 (TPT)

Dedicated

to

my daughter Raven,

son David,

(my first prayer pupils),

and Cali, my GrandGirl.

Dear Parents, Grandparents, Aunties, Uncles, and Godparents:

One of the best and lasting gifts we can give a child is teaching her or him how to communicate with the God of Creation. A child will not depart from a fervent prayer life when she or he is trained up in the way of prayer early. Teach him or her these simple prayers line by line until he or she can pray the prayer alone. You will be surprised how quickly he or she will learn them! I hope you enjoy teaching these prayers to your little one!

Morning Prayer

Good morning God

Thank you for opening my eyes to see

All the beauty You will place before me

Thank You for giving me ears to hear

I thank You that in this day, I will have no fear

As You clothe the flowers and feed the little bird

I too have all I need

because that is what is in Your Word

Thank You God for a brand new day

And for loving me in every way

In the Name of Jesus, I do pray

Amen

Mealtime Prayer

God You are great

God You are good

God I thank you for this food

I will eat, eat it all

So I can grow strong and tall

In Jesus name, Amen

Help Me Obey

Help me be good, in all I do

To be a child that pleases You

To obey my mom and my dad

And not do things that make them sad

As they train me in the right way

Help me be obedient in this day

To receive Your blessings in every way

In the Name of Jesus, I do pray

Amen

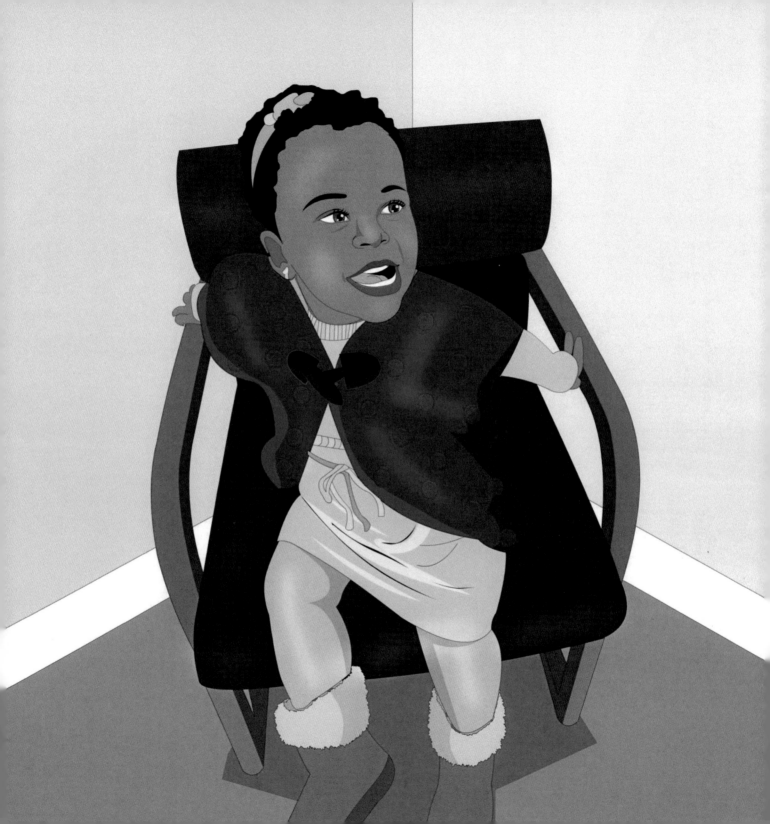

Prayer of Apology

Dear God,

Today it was hard for me to listen and obey

I was whining, pouting and wanted my way

I had a tantrum and a fit

I annoyed my mommy just a bit

Daddy questioned what all of this was about

And told me to think while in time out

Wrong behavior today I had

Making myself, mommy and daddy sad

Please forgive me

I'm sorry for my behavior today

In Jesus Name, I do pray

Amen

Bedtime Prayer

In this day, much fun I had

For everything I did, I am very glad

For a story as I prepare for bed

And a safe place to lay my head

God I thank You for all You do

No one compares to You

As I close my eyes and fall asleep

My family and me, God I ask You please keep

In the Name of Jesus, I do pray

Amen

Help Me Feel Better

A Prayer For Healing

Dear God,

I don't feel too good

I can't do the things I wish I could

I just want to run, jump, sing and play

Help me feel better so I can enjoy my day

In Jesus Name, I do pray

Amen

Prayer of Adoration

I love You Lord

Thank You for loving me

Creating me wonderfully

Helping me be all I am meant to be

I love You for giving me family who
loves me too

I love You God for all You do

In Jesus Name, Amen

Model Prayer

Our Father, who art in Heaven

Hallowed be Thy name

Thy kingdom come, Thy will be done

On earth as it is in Heaven

Give us this day our daily bread

and forgive us our trespasses

As we forgive those who trespass against us

Lead us not into temptation but deliver us from evil

For thine is the kingdom, the power and the glory,
forever and ever.

Amen

Made in the USA
Las Vegas, NV
22 January 2021